REDFIELD LIBRARY
DATE DUE

081412			
081412			
GAYLORD			PRINTED IN U.S.A.

I Can't Wait to Meet My Daddy

Written by Kathleen Blease

Illustrated by Bruce Fackenthal

Niche House
p u b l i s h i n g

A Niche House Publishing Book

Written by Kathleen Blease
Illustrated and Designed by Bruce Fackenthal
Dinosaur drawings by Ben Blease

ISBN 0-9746477-0-5

10 9 8 7 6 5 4 3 2 1

Niche House Publishing
PO Box 1954
Easton, Pennsylvania 18042
www.nichehouse.com

Other Books Coming Soon in This Series:

I Can't Wait to Meet my Grandma!
I Can't Wait to Meet my Grandpa!

Dedication

To Roger, our boys' daddy.

Introduction

You're about to become a father. A daddy. Soon the little wonder who has been filling your days (and sleepless nights) with anticipation will be in your arms warm and soft. The word *innocent* finally has meaning.

How is it this beautiful creature holds the entire future in such a tiny heart? All your hopes and dreams – all that you are, all that you ever wanted to be – asleep in your arms, a beautiful package.

Those sweet eyes will be looking to you for what the world is, or what it's supposed to be. Those delicate fingers will hold yours tightly now and, perhaps, at your final hour.

This person you helped make has never been here before, nor will be ever again. Your baby is like no other. Unique in every way. And because of this little one, your heart will be stirred, thrilled, overwhelmed, maybe even scared, and suddenly your own needs will fall away from the center of your world, replaced by your child.

Still, no matter how much you want to give your baby, there is just one thing *every* child wants: Daddy. That's you!

A daddy. What a wonderful gift to give your baby. It will last a lifetime.

Kathleen Blease

For weeks and weeks now I've been growing by leaps and bounds, from my tiny heart to my fine fingers and toes, tucked inside my warm little home. I grow and grow and stretch and kick and I know I sometimes surprise my Mommy, but I can't wait to see the world.

And most of all, I can't wait to meet my Daddy.

3

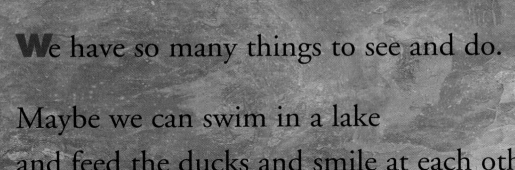

We have so many things to see and do.

Maybe we can swim in a lake
and feed the ducks and smile at each other,
then smile at the man...in the moon!

Together we must choose a name for my
teddy bear and write the alphabet from A to Z.

5

I can't wait to meet my Daddy.

I want to ask him so many things, like
why pennies are red and why cats have whiskers,
why flowers grow in the grass every Spring,
and why do worms live in the ground anyway?

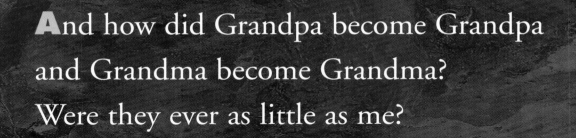

And how did Grandpa become Grandpa
and Grandma become Grandma?
Were they ever as little as me?

9

I can't wait to meet my Daddy.

He'll show me all the things I can do,
like ride a bike or a horse
or maybe even in a canoe!

11

He'll show me how to plant a tree
and fly a kite, and catch a fish,
and even, I wonder, how to ski.

13

I can't wait to meet my Daddy.

He'll teach me so many things, like adding two and two,
and making words into stories, reading the globe,
and finding starry pictures in the late, blackened night.

15

Or maybe he'll show me how to make colors that are new, like peach tree red and dinosaur lavender and daffodil green.

Then we can paint the sky.

Or maybe we can taste the sea and Daddy can
find the ocean's roar in a shell...then show me!
I must hold it to my ear just right, do you see?

21

I can't wait to meet my Daddy.

He'll love to hold me and comfort me and even sing to me (no matter how off key he may be), and he'll show me how to be brave and kind, and how to build all the things I need inside of me. Oh, I can't wait to meet my Daddy!

If I could meet him right now,
I'd ask, "Am I just like you?"

I can't wait to meet my Daddy.
I will someday very soon.

And we have oh so much to do!

I can't wait to meet my Daddy,

_____
Daddy

Let's meet on _____
due date

at _____
birth place

with _____
Mommy

Love, _____
Newborn